The CLEVELAND BROWNS
Power and Glory

The CLEVELAND BROWNS

Power and Glory

by Chuck Heaton

A Stuart L. Daniels Book

PRENTICE-HALL, INC.
Englewood Cliffs, New Jersey

Art Directors: Suzanne Esper
Renate Lude
Editorial Associate: Daniel Goldschmidt
Special Projects Director: Elizabeth J. Cossa

THE CLEVELAND BROWNS
Power and Glory

by Chuck Heaton

Copyright © 1974 by
The Stuart L. Daniels Company, Inc.

Published by Prentice-Hall, Inc.
Englewood Cliffs, New Jersey

Printed in the United States of America T
Prentice-Hall International, Inc., London
Prentice-Hall of Australia, Pty. Ltd., Sydney
Prentice-Hall of Canada, Ltd., Toronto
Prentice-Hall of India Private Ltd., New Delhi
Prentice-Hall of Japan, Inc., Tokyo

ISBN: 0-13-136754-4

Library of Congress Catalog Card Number: 74-9242

Photography by:

Timothy Culek   Russ Reed
Malcolm W. Emmons   Clifton Boutelle
Paul Tepley   John Biever
Chance Brockway   Vernon Biever

Although he gained only 369 yards rushing in 1973, fourth on the team, many experts consider Greg Pruitt to be the running back of the future for the Browns.

pruitt
can do it

Many of the spectators were nodding in their seats. In the press box the reporters were cracking jokes and telling stories, paying scant attention to the doings on the floor of the Astrodome. It was that sort of game.

It was a November afternoon in Houston in 1973 and the Browns, still hopeful of making the National Football League playoffs, were taking on a hapless Oiler team. Cleveland held a 10–0 lead in the first quarter.

Then Mike Phipps, the Browns quarterback, sent Greg Pruitt off right tackle. It was a first down play, one that should make a couple of yards.

The little rookie from Oklahoma darted through a small hole, cut to the outside and was in the clear. Sudden electricity filled the air and touched the spectators as Pruitt raced down the sideline for fifty-three yards and a touchdown.

That was just one of many exciting shows put on by the mighty little man that season. Although the Browns faded in the stretch and didn't make the playoffs 1973 could not be considered a total loss.

It probably will go down in the team's history as the year that Pruitt was discovered. Although he only weighs 185 pounds and stands about five-foot-nine in his cleats, he does a lot of things on offense and all of them very well.

As far as Browns' players go there have been three eras since the team was put together by Paul Brown in 1946. Otto Graham, a quarterback now in the Hall of Fame, dominated the first decade of play as Cleveland consistently won championships.

Then after the team's only losing season in 1956, a fellow by the name of Jim Brown was drafted out of Syracuse. He was to lead a devastating ground attack in his nine brilliant years at fullback. The team won the NFL title in 1964 and consistently remained in contention.

Brown seemed at the peak of his career in 1965. He had all the old speed and power plus the knowhow that comes with combating NFL defenses over the years. A new challenge in the shape of a film career came along and Jim called it quits.

Cleveland, however, had the right man in the wings. Leroy Kelly took over as the premier running back and the team remained highly competitive.

Graham, Brown, Kelly. With Leroy near the end of his active football career the era of Pruitt is about to begin.

Greg, a bouncy little guy whose face lights up when he talks, is the fastest of the Browns. Although clocked at under 4.5 seconds for forty yards he is more than just a straight-ahead sprinter.

Pruitt could be the best broken field runner the Browns ever have had. This, of course, makes him an excellent punt return man and he might be helped immeasurably by the new rule which should give him more running room.

Leroy Kelly, with twenty-seven 100-yard games under his belt, may be the finest running back ever to wear a Brown uniform with the exception of the greatest runner of all time, Jim Brown.

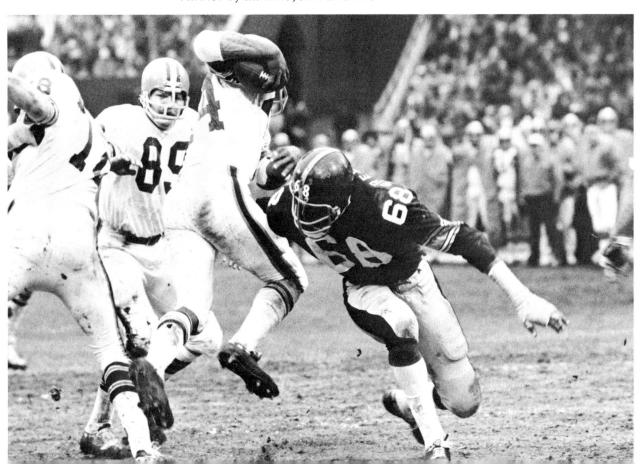

Greg also can catch the ball. And surprisingly enough, he's an excellent blocker.

The Browns had four choices in the first two rounds of the 1973 draft. The initial pick was Steve Holden, a wide receiver from Arizona State. Then they tapped Pete Adams, a guard from Southern California who had a regular job until an exhibition game injury put him out for the season.

Pruitt was grabbed as the first pick in the second round. It proved to be Cleveland's best selection of the day and one that is adding a new dimension to the Cleveland attack.

The runner-up for the 1972 Heisman Trophy, he had been a consensus All America pick with awards from most major magazines and wire services. His big year at Oklahoma was 1971 when he gained 1,665 yards.

As a college senior, Greg scored fourteen touchdowns and had a career total of forty. He went on to grab the honor of being the outstanding player in the Hula Bowl.

Pruitt was used sparingly during the early going of 1973 as he showed some tendency to fumble and was also bothered by nagging injuries. Even so, he wound up with some impressive statistics.

He was fourth in team rushing with 369 yards and a 6.1 average. He caught nine passes for 110 yards and a 12.2 average.

Greg first caught the fancy of the crowds and the eyes of the coaches with his kickoff and punt returns. He rolled back 453 yards with sixteen kickoffs and had one romp of fifty-four yards. His sixteen punt returns accounted for 180 yards and there was a dash of forty-six yards.

the paul brown era

The Cleveland Browns came into existence in 1945 when millionaire Arthur McBride decided to add a football team to his many enterprises. He offered to buy the National Football League's Cleveland Rams but his bid was refused, even though the Rams had been operating in the red.

At about the same time, Arch Ward, late sports editor of the Chicago *Tribune,* was in the process of helping form a new professional league to be called the All-America Conference. Since McBride couldn't buy a team, he decided he would start one from scratch, as part of the new league.

...aul Brown, in thirteen seasons at Cleve-
...nd's helm won seven divisional titles and
...ree league championships in the course of
...ompiling a fantastic 115–39–5 record.

Jim Brown wasn't as immense as the running backs of the 1970's, but was well known for being as solid as any player before or since his time.

After looking around, McBride hired former Ohio State coach Paul Brown. Brown, in turn, rounded up personnel for the team. He started with quarterback Otto Graham who had been with the Detroit Lions. Graham was later joined by such future greats as Mac Speedie, Dante Lavelli, Eddie Ulinski, Lou Saban, Lin Houston, Lou Rymkus and Edgar (Special Delivery) Jones. Perhaps the most important acquisition was Lou Groza, a powerful offensive tackle who became known as the game's finest kicker.

Paul Brown was the guiding genius in that period of high hopes and strong morale, so when a contest was held to choose a name for the team, the "Browns" was selected as a tribute to the head coach.

Shortly afterwards the Cleveland Rams moved to Los Angeles, hoping for better attendance and greater local support at their games. Thus Cleveland was left to the Browns, and the citizens of Cleveland now had a winning team. In the entire four years of the All-America Conference's existence, Cleveland won the championship each year and lost only four games.

After the demise of the All-America Conference, the Browns joined the National Football League and continued to play like champions. Their only losing season in that period was in 1956, after Otto Graham retired. By 1957, however, they were back in the playoffs, thanks to a fullback named Jim Brown.

An All-Pro for almost as many years as he ias played professional football, Jim Brown vas inducted into the Pro Football Hall of Tame in 1971.

art modell takes over

In 1961, at a time when it seemed that the era of the glorious Browns would never end, the Cleveland team was bought by a group headed by Arthur B. Modell, a New York advertising executive and avid football fan with outstanding business acumen. He paid over $4,000,000 for the Cleveland team, and although, at the time, there were those who doubted the wisdom of the purchase, the club is now worth many times that figure.

Knowing full well that one of the key factors in the Browns' success was coach Paul Brown himself, Modell quickly agreed to the long-term contract for which Brown asked and which would guarantee the continuance of his almost unlimited power over team policy. There were many outward signs of warmth and mutual respect at the start of this relationship, but it wasn't too long before seeds of discord began to sprout.

Gary Collins, the leading receiver Browns' history, had an illustrious lo career at Cleveland.

Former outstanding Cleveland safety Ross Fichtner had eight strong seasons with the Browns.

No essential rapport was established between Modell and Brown and no true lines of communication existed. Brown made major decisions without consulting Modell, some of which turned out to be serious errors.

The Browns finished the 1962 season 7–6–1, their poorest record since 1956. Modell wasn't pleased, and it was rumored that Brown, football institution though he might be, was going to be fired. Modell's disappointment was echoed by many of the players who were dissatisfied with what they believed to be Brown's faltering leadership.

Exit Paul Brown

In the opening weeks of 1963, Art Modell announced that Paul Brown was being relieved of his duties as coach and general manager. His long-term contract, which called for payment of over $80,000 a year, would be honored, but his activities would be confined to special scouting assignments. The new coach, Blanton Collier, met with the players' approval, but it was clear that Art Modell was now going to be the strong man and key decision maker.

Art Modell has often initiated trades (with the approval of his coaches). He is active in league affairs and has served as president of the National Football League. One of his most important decisions occurred during the merger talks between the two leagues in 1969. He broke the deadlock over realignment of teams by agreeing to move Cleveland to what had formerly been the American Football League, along with Pittsburgh and Baltimore. That move gave the NFL its present setup of thirteen teams in the National Football Conference and thirteen teams in the American Football Conference.

Like many team owners, Modell's greatest ambition is to be a Super Bowl winner. Although he can be proud that the Browns have fairly consistently made the playoffs, up through 1973 they had yet to move beyond the semi-final playoff round. But Art Modell continues to plan and to fight and, hopefully, to finally win the elusive trophy.

Gene Hickerson is a six-time All-Pro.

Paul Brown was the guiding force in the Cleveland franchise for almost two decades.

Fred Hoaglin (54) was a linebacker during the heyday of the Browns in the late 1950's.

coach nick skorich

...nce becoming head coach at Cleveland, ...ck Skorich has led the Browns to a ...–14–2 record.

In the Brown's twenty-eight year history they have had only three head coaches. The first, of course, was Paul Brown, a founder of the team whose exploits have ensconced him in professional football's Hall of Fame.

When Brown left Cleveland early in 1963, he was followed by a former disciple, Blanton Collier. Collier proved to be a worthy choice. In his first season (1963) the Browns achieved a 10–4 record. The following year, led by the topnotch play of Jim Brown, Frank Ryan, and Gary Collins, Cleveland swept the Eastern Conference title and followed it with a 27–0 upset over the Baltimore Colts to win the National Football League championship. Collier followed with five more winning seasons including Eastern Conference championships in 1968 and 1969.

Former quarterback Bill Nelsen hands off to Bo Scott, who appears to have a good deal of running room.

At the end of 1970, which the Browns ended with a 7–7 record, only the second time in their history that they had not won more games than they lost, Collier asked to be relieved. Today, in semi-retirement, he scouts the southeast for the team.

A less than satisfactory record for a team with such a powerful past seemed to call for new thoughts and new directions. Thus it was that Nick Skorich took the reins as coach in January, 1971. Along with a three-year contract he was given full control of the team.

The Brown's ended the 1971 season with a 9–5 mark and as champions of the American Football Conference's Central Division. Nineteen-seventy-two's record of 10–4 and the "wild card" playoff berth indicated to the powers that be that Nick Skorich was definitely on the right track. Even though only two years had passed, his contract was rewritten for three more years.

A Coaching Career

Nick Skorich had played football as a guard at the University of Cincinnati, following which he spent three years with the Pittsburgh Steelers. In addition to playing ball he managed to obtain a masters degree. However, he was heading for a career in coaching.

At first Skorich coached high school and college teams, and then, from 1954 to 1957, put in a stint as line coach for the Steelers. The next year he moved to Green Bay as both the over-all offensive coach and coach of the offensive line. In 1959 he went to Philadelphia to take charge of the Eagles' running game. When Buck Shaw retired at the end of the 1960 season, Skorich replaced him as the Eagles' head coach.

After missing repeating as Eastern Conference champions by one-half game in 1961, the Eagle went 6–20–3 the next two seasons under Skorich. Though injuries and organizational problems were abundant, Skorich, as head coach, took the brunt of the blame. He was fired after 1963, but not without testimonials from a number of his former players. Additional reassurances about his capabilities came in the form of excellent offers of coaching jobs from other NFL teams.

The two opposing lines—immobile before the snap of the ball.

The interior line of Cleveland—the heart of a successful team.

The Browns' present coach has a friendly manner but also is known as a disciplinarian. He runs a tight ship and isn't afraid to take action when necessary. He showed that he meant business immediately after taking the reins of the Browns with a reorganization of the coaching staff.

With the team slipping to a dismal mark of seven victories, five defeats and two ties in 1973, he felt that another overhaul was in order. This one was even more sweeping.

Gone from the 1974 staff are Howard Brinker, the coach of overall defense and a staff member for 22 years; offensive backfield coach John David Crow who shifted to the San Diego Chargers and Jerry Smith who tutored the offensive line for one season.

Richie McCabe, a vibrant man with bright ideas and the willingness to express them, had been overseeing the defensive backs. He has taken charge of the defense. Dale Lindsay who retired as a player at the end of the 1973 season, moved in as linebacker coach.

The two new faces on offense are Dick Wood, a one-time quarterback for the New York Jets, before the Joe Namath era, and Forrest Gregg, who gained fame and fortune on the offensive line of the Green Bay Packers.

Wood has plans for more than minor tinkering with the offense. Gregg is in charge of completing the rebuilding of the offensive line. Al Tabor has the duty of directing the running backs, in addition to continuing as coach of the special teams.

Dick Modzelewski signed a two-year contract to continue as defensive line coach. Fran Polsfoot remained as coach of the receivers.

Skorich gives his aides a lot of freedom in their particular areas. However, there is no doubt about who runs the team. When decisions are made, they are made by Nick Skorich.

Thus, the head coach is squarely on the spot in the coming seasons. Obviously some of the blame for the unhappy 1973 showing had been put at the door of the assistant coaches.

Skorich hand-picked his new people, with the approval of Modell. Results are now expected and the head coach will be held responsible. The owner and the fans are looking forward to a resurgence of the Browns.

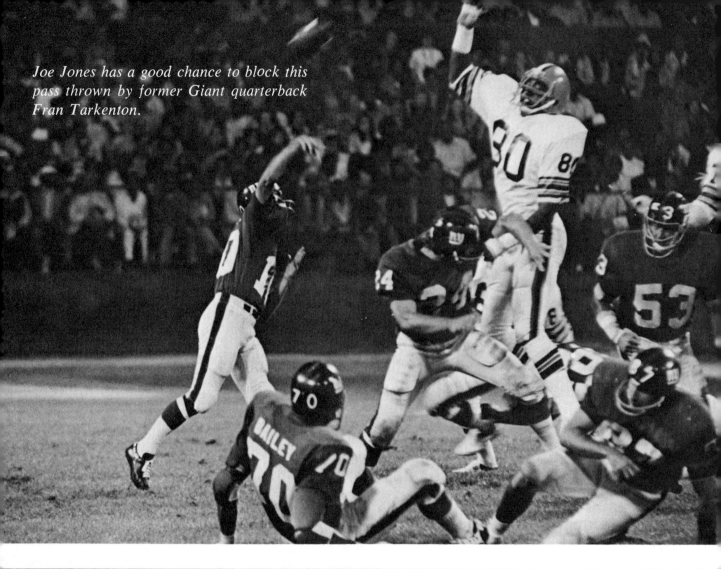

Joe Jones has a good chance to block this pass thrown by former Giant quarterback Fran Tarkenton.

ver the years, the Browns and the Giants
ve met many times in epic confrontations
 the gridiron. A fierce rivalry between
e two teams has resulted.

(Left to right) Jim Houston, Walter Johnson, Jerry Sherk, and Bo Cornell get set to block on a kick return.

Members of the Browns' defense in action.

an optimistic outlook

There was an air of optimism in July of 1973 as the Browns gathered at their longtime training quarters at quiet, picturesque Hiram College, a thirty-five-mile drive from downtown Cleveland. Coach Nick Skorich greeted reporters with a wide smile. Morrie Kono, the veteran equipment manager, beamed as he fitted pads and handed out fatherly advice, and trainer Leo Murphy noted with approval the husky newcomers.

It was a far cry from the previous year—the summer of 1972—when things started out badly and began to go downhill. Then, defensive end Jack Gregory had just defected to the New York Giants after playing out his option.

Mitch Johnson and Joe Righetti, two experienced tackles, were missing. Wide receiver Gary Collins, a brilliant clutch performer during the Blanton Collier era, had called it a career. He was a victim of age and the bumping tactics of defensive backs.

All of these things added up. There was also the problem of working in Mike Phipps at quarterback. It's little wonder that the club lost all its exhibition games and began the regular season as the longest of long shots to gain the National Football League playoffs.

The Browns did just that with a rousing late season comeback, however, and went on to scare mighty Miami in the first of the post season games. They lost to the Dolphins but in a manner that convinced everybody from Art Modell to the lowliest rookie that this was a team with a future—a possible Super Bowl contender.

The outlook seemed bright but Skorich added a note of caution as he greeted the squad. The coach admitted that he thought the club was on the upswing but warned that it would take continuous and complete dedication.

The Browns were in the East Division in the American Conference. So were, and are, the Pittsburgh Steelers and the Cincinnati Bengals. Skorich noted that both of these teams were young and improving. He suggested that the Browns would have to get better to keep pace.

The coach always believed in bringing his squad along slowly in the summer campaigning, but losing all six exhibition games in 1972 was too much.

While the Browns didn't do a complete turnabout in 1973 they weren't wiped out. After an opening loss to the San Francisco 49ers, they headed west to tie the Los Angeles Rams.

Then came victories over the Bengals and the Atlanta Falcons before windup defeats at the hands of the Detroit Lions and the New York Giants. The victory over Atlanta proved costly, however, as Pete Adams, who seemed to have a starting guard post nailed down in this rookie try, suffered a knee injury requiring surgery that would sideline him for the season.

Bill Nelsen had retired from playing to take a job as quarterback coach of the New England Patriots. So Phipps no longer had the veteran looking over his shoulder and there was no question about the identity of the Cleveland signal caller. A new backup man was Don Horn, obtained from the Denver Broncos in a winter trade.

Two Browns converge on the "Bowling Ball," Baltimore running back Don Nottingham.

The Cleveland offense moves to the left to block, as Phipps hands off to his fullback, Leroy Kelly.

Mike Phipps is just a sleeve away from a touchdown and has the end zone in sight in this 1972 playoff action against Miami.

A Good Start

There were other injuries as the opener against the Baltimore Colts at Cleveland Stadium approached but the Browns did get one break. Bert Jones, a rookie, was nominated to start for the visitors and the Cleveland defense looked forward with great expectation to initiating the young quarterback into pro football.

Jones was pressured unmercifully as the Browns went on to a 24–14 victory before 74,303 partisans. The son of former Cleveland star Dub Jones was thrown five times for losses of fifty-two yards and had one pass intercepted.

It was a victory but not very impressive. The Browns had fumbled away the ball three times and watched the Colts turn a blocked punt into a touchdown.

Next on the agenda were the Steelers, in Pittsburgh's Three Rivers Stadium. Few visiting teams have had much success there and the Browns embarked on their charter flight with some trepidation.

The gasoline crunch kept the usual mob of fans from making the 150-mile trip down the Ohio and Pennsylvania turnpikes to see the game but a few did get there. The lucky ones were those who remained at home and could turn off their television sets.

Cleveland lost by a 33–6 count and it wasn't a game that needed analyzing. The Steelers were superior in every department and the Browns were simply overwhelmed by a better football team.

So it was back to Cleveland for some regrouping before meeting the Giants. It was expected that the New York club would be in an aggressive mood as it had been tied by the Philadelphia Eagles the previous week.

The Browns were underdogs at the kickoff and it looked as though the oddsmakers were right when the visitors to Lake Erie jumped out to a 10–0 halftime lead. That was all they managed, however, and Cleveland rallied with four field goals by Don Cockroft after the intermission, for a 12–10 victory.

It wasn't a particularly impressive victory but it was an important one. The Browns had regained respectability.

In 1973, Leroy Kelly rushed for 381 yards, giving him 7,274 yards lifetime, fourth on the career rushing list.

Ken Brown cuts upfield with a kick.

Cleveland sportswriters now had some kind words for the 1973 team. The defense had been a stone wall in the second half against the Giants and much praise was heaped on the unit for a gutsy job.

A late trade with San Diego brought Bob Bavich to the Browns. It took a heavy toll in draft choices to get the middle linebacker but he quickly moved in as a regular and the leader of the defense. The swap loomed even more important when it was learned that Billy Andrews, slated to be the regular middle backer, had a back problem. Surgery shelved him for the season.

The next opponent was Cincinnati. There always has been something special about this rivalry because of ex-Cleveland coach Paul Brown who now runs the Bengals. Each team also needed a victory in the division race which intensified the day's activity.

It was time for the Browns much maligned offensive line to come alive. After Cleveland's 17–10 victory, Brown said, "Certainly, the better team won."

Bob Johnson, veteran center of the Bengals, put it this way—"The offensive team of the Browns made zero mistakes." It had been a big day for Phipps who did a first rate job of play calling.

There was no time for celebration. Next visitors to Cleveland were the Miami Dolphins. They well recalled the scare the Browns had given them in the playoffs nine months earlier and they weren't about to be taken by surprise.

The Cleveland attack went sour in this Monday night game. The defense gave up only seventeen points but finally was worn down by the running of Larry Csonka. The Browns points came on three field goals by Cockroft.

The way the Browns were playing it didn't seem that any team could provide a breather. The Houston Oilers, however, did just that. Cleveland was ahead by twenty-eight points at the half and coasted to a 42–13 victory.

Greg Pruitt got into the ball carrying act in this one and averaged 5.1 yards on eleven carries. There were indications that he soon would be taking much of the burden from the veteran Leroy Kelly.

"Bo is a punishing runner," says Nick Skorich of his young running back.

Behind the blocking of Joe Carollo (63) and Jim Copeland (64), Leroy Kelly can count on a good gain on this play.

A Four-Two Record

With the halfway mark of the campaign coming up things looked brighter for the Browns. They had a 4–2 record and expected to beat the visiting Chargers who, at times, seemed almost as hapless as the Oilers.

Perhaps the Browns let down. Perhaps they were over-confident. Whatever the reason, they played poorly against the California club and trailed through much of the game. Pruitt found the end zone from six yards out late in the fourth quarter to put the Browns ahead but the joy on the lakefront was of short duration.

Cleveland's defense, sturdy for so long, crumbled in the closing minutes and San Diego worked down the field for the tying field goal. The score was 16–16. Now the Browns had a 4–2–1 record with the tougher half of the schedule coming up and six of the seven games on the road.

The travels began with a swing into Bloomington for a game against the Vikings. All four starters on the Cleveland defensive line had been down with the flu during the week and there was much concern about being able to keep up with the scrambling Fran Tarkenton.

That defense did reasonably well but the attack got only a field goal in the 26–3 defeat.

There was a good deal of soul searching the week after that defeat. Modell said he felt it was a time for a thorough analysis by everybody and he huddled with Skorich and his staff. There were complaints from the fans and writers about Phipps' performance and the view was expressed that Bill Nelsen should have been kept as a quarterback coach.

Houston was next on the program and there wasn't a better foe in the NFL to bounce back against. The Browns didn't distinguish themselves in that visit to the Astrodome but a fifty-three-yard touchdown dash by Pruit provided the spark in the 23–13 triumph.

So it was on to Oakland and a game against the Raiders. Oakland was fighting for a division title, too, and was rated extremely strong at home.

Defensive end Joe Jones was out the ent 1972 season with an injury.

Chip Glass is an excellent reserve tight end and gives the Browns added strength at that position.

The Browns took the lead early in the second quarter when Phipps got Fair Hooker one-on-one in the end zone. He lobbed a pass over the head of veteran defensive back Willie Brown.

Raider quarterback Ken Stabler was cracked to the ground five times on a superb showing by the foursome of Joe Jones, Nick Roman, Walter Johnson and Jerry Sherk.

Oakland couldn't even take advantage of five Cleveland fumbles. George Blanda's fourth quarter field goal provided the Raiders' only points in Cleveland's 7–3 triumph.

Beating the Steelers

Immediately after the game the Browns flew home to prepare for a visit by the Steelers.

The Steelers scored first on a pass from Joe Gilliam to Ron Shanklin after starting quarterback Terry Hanratty of Pittsburgh had gone to the bench with damaged ribs. Phipps sneaked a yard to tie it for Cleveland and Pruitt took a fifteen-yard pass from Mike for a touchdown that put the Browns ahead.

Roy Gerela moved the Steelers within one point with a pair of field goals and then into the lead in the fourth quarter with a twenty-yard kick.

There were four minutes and ten seconds remaining when linebacker John Garlington recovered a fumble by Gilliam on the Cleveland thirty-nine-yard line. Two running plays failed to gain. Then Phipps, flushed from the pocket, seemed to evade the whole Steeler defense before locating Pruitt who was loose downfield for a gain to the Pittsburgh eighteen-yard line. That was the season's most spectacular play, the kind that draws people to the game.

Kelly lost a yard before Pruitt again took over. This time the rookie swept around left end for nineteen yards and a touchdown. The Browns won, 21–16.

erry Sherk (72) and Walter Johnson (71)
re the leaders of the Browns' defensive
ne.

Cornerback Ben Davis (28) has the know-how and talent to make the perfect tackle. Cincinnati's Chip Myers would probably agree.

Ken Brown steadies himself after a near tackle and eyes other potential Giant defenders.

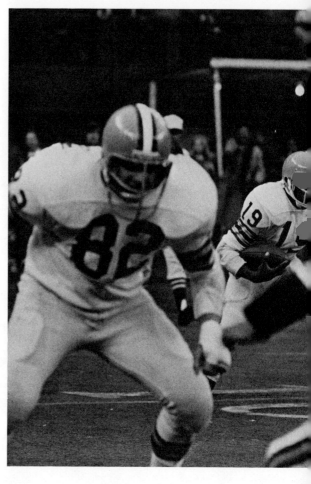

Jim Houston is ready to meet the challenge of Bengals' Bernard Jackson on this kickoff return by Billy Lefear (background).

It took a sixty-five-yard dash by Pruitt and a dramatic fifty-one-yard pass from Phipps to Milt Morin for touchdowns that tied Kansas City at 20–all. Then the team ran out of steam resulting in defeats—34–17 to Cincinnati and 30–17 to Los Angeles.

A lot caught up with the Browns as they faded in the stretch. One was the schedule, the final six of seven games on the road against formidable opposition—an almost impossible task.

There were injuries, too. Some were serious and others, the nagging kind that doesn't put a man on the bench but impairs his efficiency. There was also the slowing down of some older players and the slower-than-anticipated development of others.

High Hopes

Skorich, however, found much to cheer about as he added up the pluses and minuses for the season. Pruitt had gradually come of age during the season as he worked into a more prominent role with the team. Future stardom seemed assured for him.

Phipps took some steps forward and some backward all season but progress was made. He should be ready to take complete charge in 1974 and beyond, when some of the new rules limiting the defense should help his style of play.

Pete Adams' recovery from a knee injury seems to have been complete and he should take over the guard job held by the retired Gene Hickerson.

Improvement in performance from the other younger players such as offensive tackle Doug Dieken, defensive backs Thom Darden and Clarence Scott as well as Van Green is expected. After a year with the team and knee surgery, Bob Babich should do much better at middle linebacker and he was first rate in 1973. Charlie Hall has made steady progress as an outside backer.

Billy Andrews won't let go of Pittsburgh's Franco Harris.

ill Andrews seems to enjoy the sport of ccer on occasion.

hn Demarie (65) and Leroy Kelly run to position to block for Mike Phipps.

There are strong indications that the fans will see an improved offense with a much better running game. No deterioration in defense is expected and the presence of Don Cockroft assures a solid kicking game.

There is high hope that Billy Pritchett, a king-sized fullback from West Texas State, will help the running game.

Skorich remains optimistic about the future of the Browns. He feels that some of the 1973 problems were caused by the youthfulness of the club but he believes that this, in the long run, will prove a tremendous asset.

The Central Division of the AFC is getting better all the time and the Browns must improve to stay competitive. The coach is confident this is happening.

In any event a club that features Greg Pruitt should be interesting to watch.

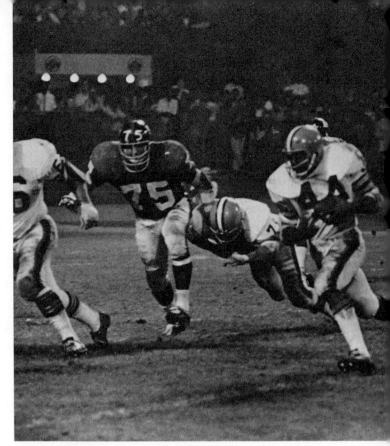

Milt Morin (89) and Chris Morris hold off a Lion pass rush.

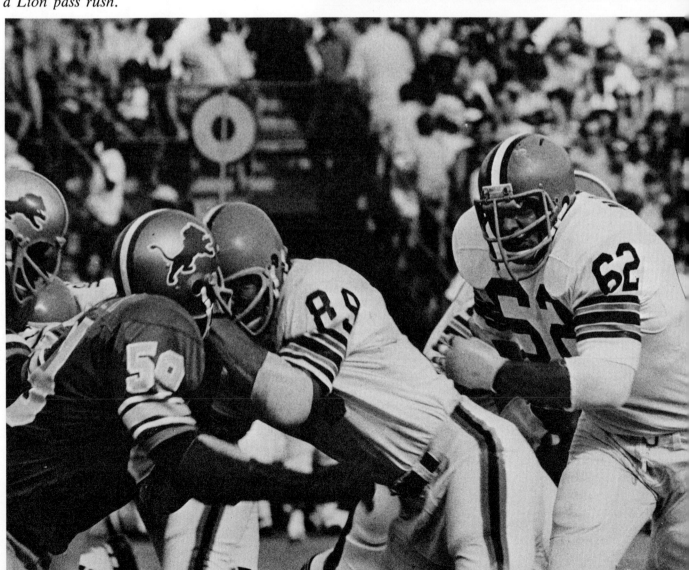

Leroy Kelly is on his way with a handoff from Bill Nelsen and some good blocking from the line.

Wide receiver Fair Hooker has improved more rapidly in a few years than have most players in football.

Cleveland's Bob Briggs wants the fumble, but so do the Giants, and Bob is outnumbered five to one.

Leroy Kelly sweeps around a fallen mass of players—both friend and foe.

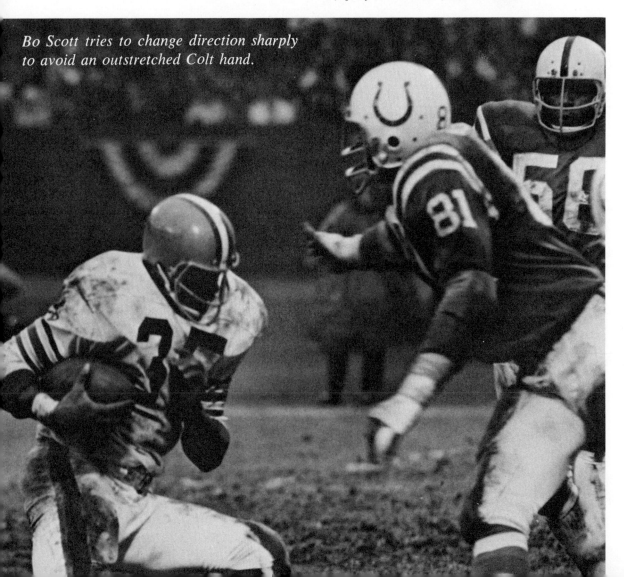

Bo Scott tries to change direction sharply to avoid an outstretched Colt hand.

Safety Walt Sumner reaches for Elmo Wright, Kansas City Chief wide receiver, after a pass reception.

The offensive line gives Bo Scott good blocking against a talented Bengal defense.

the browns--

brains and brawn

leroy kelly

The Browns were headed downfield during the game with the Cincinnati Bengals in December 1972. They needed yardage and points, so, naturally, the ball was handed to Leroy Kelly. Leroy took the handoff from Mike Phipps and shot through the line for eleven yards. A few moments later Don Cockroft booted an easy field goal for the 27–24 victory.

That run was more than just another solid gain for Kelly, however. The yardage lifted him ahead of John Henry Johnson on the National Football League's all-time rushing list. Leroy finished the 1972 season with 811 yards and a career total of 6,885 yards, making him the fourth most productive ball carrier in league history. Kelly seems to be carrying on the tradition of top rusher Jim Brown.

When Jim Brown retired before the 1966 season to pursue a film career, there were dire predictions about the Browns' running game. One man who wasn't upset was Dub Jones, then offensive backfield coach.

"Kelly is going to surprise a lot of people," declared Dub. "He's a fine running back and can do a lot of things. He's not as big as Brown but he'll get the job done."

Dub turned out to be right. Leroy rolled up 1,141 yards in that first season as a regular and went over 1,200 yards in each of the next two years.

Kelly, an eighth-round draft choice out of Morgan State, was used mostly as a kick-return specialist during his first two years. He began the 1973 season with predictions that it would be his last. The thirty-one-year-old veteran reflected, "Now I'm in my tenth season and at the end of another contract. My feeling is that this will be my last contract and my last year. Physically, I probably could play two or three more years, as I've been fortunate and haven't had any knee trouble. I think I'll be satisfied with ten years, though."

Leroy Kelly had the difficult job of succeeding the legendary Jim Brown, but has more than made his mark on football in Cleveland.

Although he is often tired during a gam[e] Leroy Kelly is seldom too worn out to back in for his team.

His unquestioned pass-catching ability is shown as Leroy Kelly latches onto a pass

The hard life of a pro running back: Even the best must suffer, as Leroy Kelly, bruised, battered and mud-streaked, lies forlornly on the turf.

mike phipps

The quarterback is a key man on any football team. This is certainly the case with Mike Phipps, who moved in as the regular in 1972 and led the Browns to the play-offs. He continued in that role in 1973.

There have been some good quarterbacks on the Browns since Otto Graham decided to end his career following the 1955 season, but Phipps seems to have the combination of physical and mental equipment to be the best since Cleveland's Hall of Famer.

At six-foot-three and 208 pounds, Phipps doesn't have a sprinter's speed but he does a good job of running with the football. That's attested to by his 256 yards and 4.2 average in his first starting season.

In contrast to extrovert Bill Nelsen, who led the team until Mike took over, Phipps is quiet. Once he was handed the starting job, however, he took charge and the players respect him as the offensive leader.

Mike has the strength to throw the long ball, and this has tended to loosen up opposing defenses. He likes to go deep early in the game and feels this helps the shorter passes as well as the ground attack,

Coach Skorich feels that Phipps improved about fifty percent in 1972 and came on more in 1973. He is quick to add, however, that Mike will have to refine his performance which he seems to be doing. Skorich points out Phipps' tendency to run too much at times. That is a matter of experience, Skorich feels, as is reading defenses and calling plays.

Phipps was born on November 19, 1947, in Shelbyville, Indiana. He played football at Purdue, where he started in twenty-seven games, winning all but five. In one game, against Stanford, he completed twenty-eight of thirty-nine passes for 424 yards. He set twenty-four Purdue career, season, single-game and Big Ten records and was runner-up for the Heisman Trophy in 1969.

Phipps is considered to be one of the fine young prospects in the NFL. He carries the hopes of the Browns for the next decade on his broad shoulders.

Quarterback Mike Phipps was a star student and athlete at Purdue.

Quarterback Mike Phipps prepares to hand off to Leroy Kelly.

Phipps turns to hand off to a running back.

Mike Phipps drops back to pass as his offensive linemen, tackle Joe Carollo (63), guards Gene Hickerson (66) and John Demarie (65), and tackle Bob McKay (78) form a perfect protective pocket to give him time to throw.

jerry sherk

The Browns believe they have the best pair of defensive tackles in football. One is Walter Johnson. The other is young Jerry Sherk, who is still improving at that position.

Despite the injuries which plagued Cleveland's defensive squad, their defense remained reasonably solid in 1972. Johnson and Sherk were the fellows who kept things on an even keel.

Sherk was the Browns' only rookie starter in the 1970 season. He continues to improve and should soon be rated with the best in the National Football League.

Sherk was born in Grants Pass, Oregon and went to Oklahoma State where he gained a national reputation as a collegiate wrestler.

He was drafted in the second round in 1970. His progress was swift that summer, so fast that the Browns felt they could trade Marv Upshaw to the Kansas City Chiefs for a draft choice. That pick was used to select linebacker Charlie Hall.

Sherk puts a lot of pressure on the passer. He also has good lateral pursuit along the line. In fact, he has come a long way from the little guy who tried out in junior high school at quarterback, weighing 141 pounds. Things went so poorly that he gave up the sport until his senior year in high school.

With Sherk and Johnson as the mainstays, the Browns just might have one of the best defensive lines in the business.

Jerry Sherk moves in quickly on Cincinnati running back Jess Phillips.

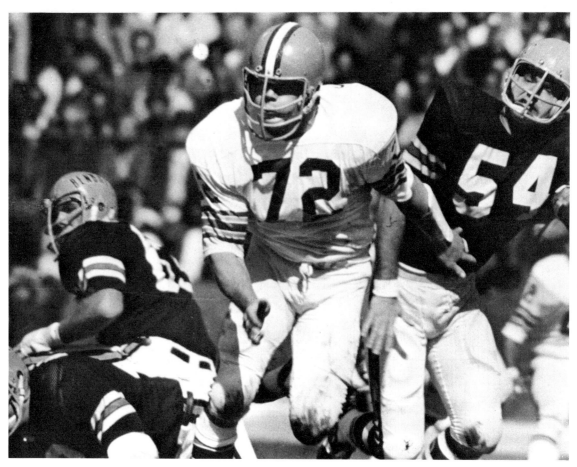

Defensive tackle Jerry Sherk splits the Bengal offensive line as he charges in on the Bengal quarterback.

Defensive tackle Jerry Sherk wades through a pile of bodies to reach the Bengal ball-carrier, who is about to be tackled.

Nick Roman has his arms around the Bengal ballcarrier as an eager and intense Jerry Sherk rushes in to help his teammate and complete the tackle.

Defensive tackle Jerry Sherk pulls down Cincinnati's Essex Johnson.

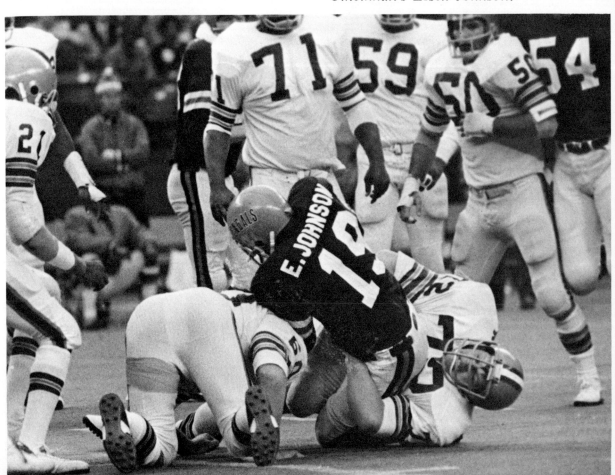

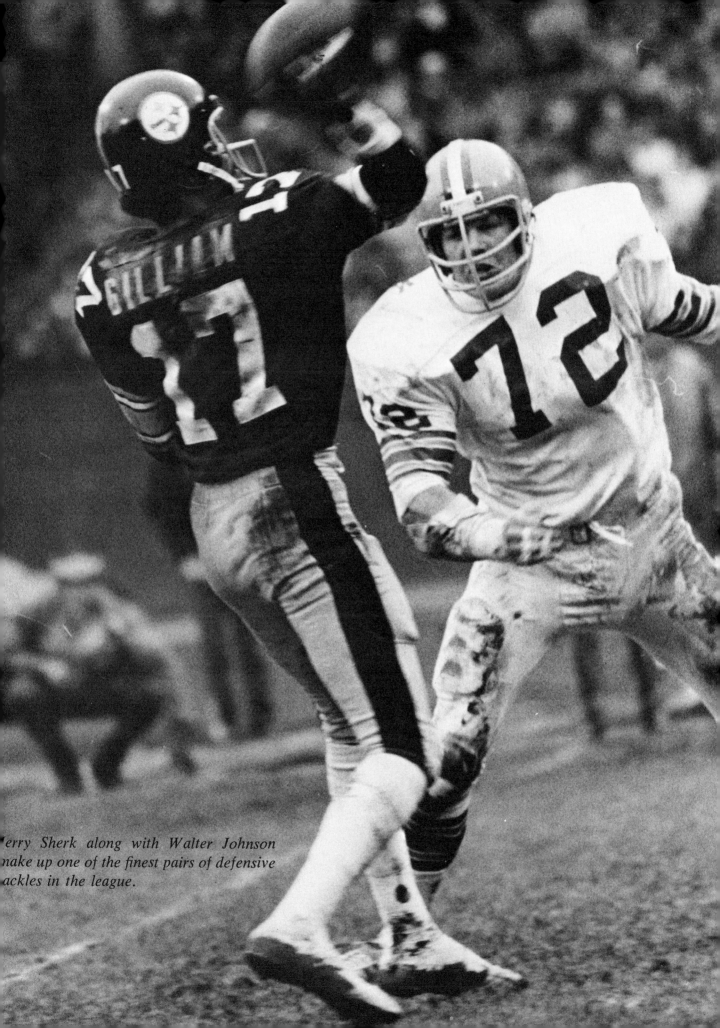

*erry Sherk along with Walter Johnson
nake up one of the finest pairs of defensive
ackles in the league.*

walter johnson

There are a lot of people in the Cleveland area, Coach Nick Skorich included, who feel that the Browns' big defensive tackle, Walter Johnson, doesn't get his share of the honors. Johnson, who has played eight seasons of professional football in Cleveland, has been a stalwart on the line.

He grew up in Cincinnati but played college football at California State in Los Angeles. Although he has been on three Pro Bowl teams, he never made All-Pro. But Johnson's contribution to the Cleveland squad is significant.

His strength is against the running game and he's sometimes referred to as the "policeman" of the defensive line.

"Walter keeps our front four together," says Nick Skorich. "He anchors the line and covers up for the mistakes of others. He is not a flashy player but he gives a real solid performance week after week."

Johnson had to learn the defensive tackle spot after he joined the Browns. He was a fullback during his football years at Taft High School in Cincinnati, and in college he played guard and middle linebacker.

Walter backstopped Dick Modzelewski as a rookie in 1965 and then stepped in as the regular when Mo retired the next season. Dick, now defensive line coach, is highly pleased with his protegé.

"I rate Walter with the top defensive tackles," declares Mo. "He is consistent, has good speed and is quick as well as being strong. All in all, he does a first-rate job."

"Walter Johnson keeps our front four to-gether," says head coach Nick Skorich. "He anchors the line and covers up for the mis-takes of others."

Vastly underrated by everyone except opposing head coaches, Walter Johnson is one of the strongest defensive tackles in pro football. Here he breaks down the protection of the 49ers' famed offensive line and is about to sack quarterback John Brodie.

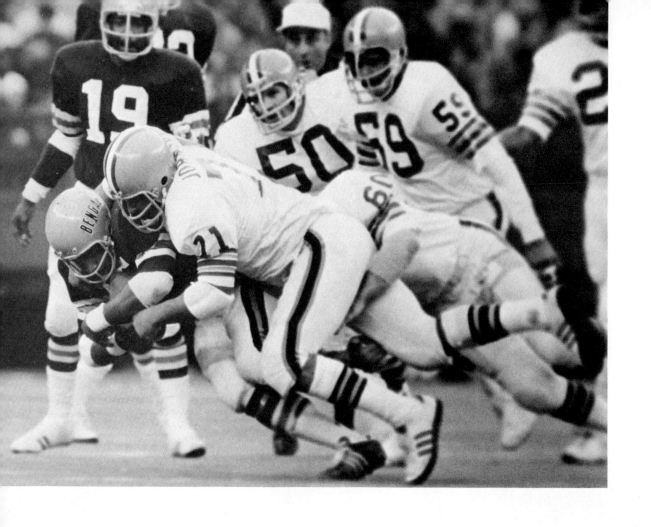

Walter Johnson applies a forearm to the hand of Bengals' Jess Phillips, who finds himself in an unenviable position.

Quick and sure-handed in 1972, Walter Johnson accomplished the lineman's dream: He intercepted a pass in the Browns' final game against the Jets.

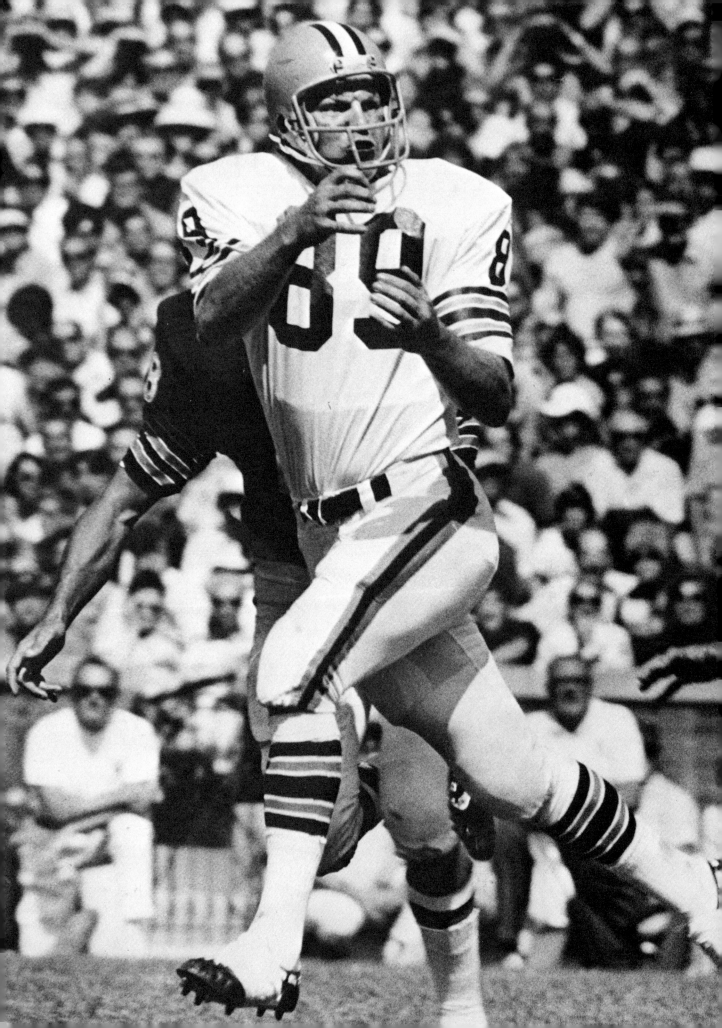

milt morin

Tight end Milt Morin runs with the ball like there's no tomorrow. Perhaps that's because in June 1969 it appeared that might be true for him. That spring there was a big question whether he would be playing any more football. In fact, there was doubt whether or not he'd ever walk again.

Flattened by the pain from a herniated disc in his lower back, the former University of Massachusetts star had to undergo surgery. It was the kind of operation that often means the end of a career. But the operation was a success and Morin surprised everyone by being able to start the 1969 regular season.

Perhaps football means even more to him now after his close escape from being sidelined in the middle of his career. He is one of the most dedicated players on the Browns' squad and the payoff has been in passes caught, yards gained and in the resulting honors.

Morin, six-foot-four and 236 pounds, twice made the Pro Bowl, and was the choice of the Cleveland Touchdown Club as offensive player of the year in 1971.

"He's a devastating man in the secondary," said Nick Skorich. "Milt runs like a wild bull on a rampage once he gets that football."

Morin was the Browns' first draft choice for 1966. His selection for the College All-Star squad slowed him down, but he soon caught up after joining the team. He also had to demonstrate willpower in another area.

The husky blond was up to 280 pounds at one time and in danger of eating himself out of the game. On orders of Blanton Collier, then head coach, Morin lost forty pounds.

An invaluable member of the squad, Milt Morin plans to play football for several more years before retiring to become proprietor of a country store on Cape Cod.

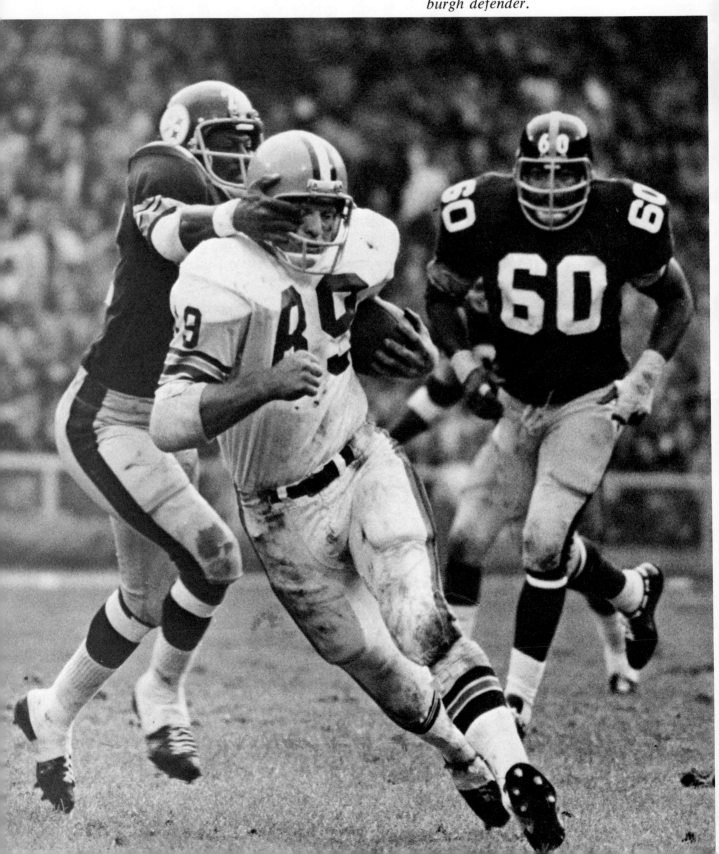

Milt Morin, one of the best veteran tight ends in the league, holds onto his reception in spite of some interference by a Pittsburgh defender.

Milt Morin, one of the leading receivers in the Browns' history, fights off an opposing defender and avoids being tackled.

Milt Morin, an All-Pro and former first-round draft pick, is one of three or four best tight ends in pro football.

Tight end Milt Morin runs "like a wild bull
on a rampage" once he gets the football,
according to head coach Nick Skorich.

bob demarco

When Jim Copeland suffered a dislocated hip early in the 1972 season, the center's job went to Fred Hoaglin. Nick Skorich decided that he needed backup help at the position and went shopping.

After numerous telephone calls and a great deal of bargaining, the services of Bob DeMarco were obtained. It proved to be one of the best deals the club ever made.

DeMarco took over at center after the Browns had been shut out by the Chicago Bears. It wasn't entirely a coincidence that the team streaked out to six straight victories and wrapped up a playoff spot with DeMarco over the ball.

DeMarco's strength lies in a combination of speed and experience. His vast knowledge of the game is the result of twelve years as a pro lineman.

"The center is the key in blocking to the right or left," said DeMarco. "If the center snaps and then moves, there is no way he is able to block his man. The guy would be past you before you raised up."

The former University of Dayton player fires out almost before the quarterback grabs the snap. It's a technique he found very useful against the odd-man defenses used by many clubs in the American Football Conference.

DeMarco was All-NFL in 1963, 1965 and 1967 while with St. Louis, and was named to the Pro Bowl in those years. Ray Prochaska was his coach for the first five years in St. Louis and the two were reunited with the Browns. Now he'll be working under Forrest Gregg.

He was called out of retirement by Skorich as he approached his mid-thirties. His decision to join the Cleveland team was a happy one for all concerned.

Bob DeMarco lends many years of experience to the difficult position of center.

Bob DeMarco performs a difficult and unrewarding job: fighting off the NFL's premier defensive tackle, Mean Joe Greene of Pittsburgh.

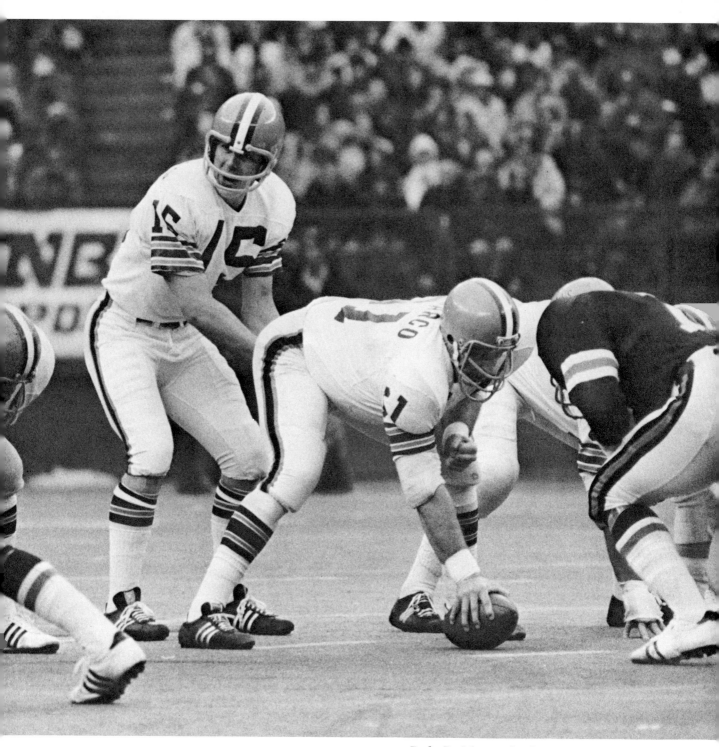

Bob DeMarco lends many years of experience to the difficult position of center.

clarence scott

ter only two years in the pro ranks, arence Scott, former All-American from nsas State, has quickly blossomed into outstanding defensive back and an chor of Cleveland's highly effective pass fense.

When the Browns took Clarence Scott as their first draft choice in 1971, the man from Kansas State declared his ambition: he hoped to become the best cornerback in football.

Scott hasn't reached his goal yet, but he's been a regular since he joined the Browns. In 1972 he was part of the top pass defensive backfield in the AFC.

Clarence, who is on the slim side at six feet and 180 pounds, was picked for the College All-Star team. This meant that he missed most of the fundamental work at training camp, but he took over the left corner in the second quarter of Cleveland's opening exhibition game. That was the end of the trail for the veteran Erich Barnes and the beginning of the pro career for the rookie.

As was expected, Scott had some first year problems. He didn't lose the starting job, however, and as a result was much better as a sophomore.

As a rookie, Scott got off to a flashy start. He had four interceptions in the first four games but went the last ten without another steal.

Scott scored Cleveland's first touchdown of the 1972 season. When defensive tackle Jerry Sherk blocked a field goal try by Green Bay, Clarence grabbed the ball in mid-air and raced fifty-five yards for the touchdown.

He made the Pro Bowl squad in 1973.

The young Cleveland star was co-captain at Kansas State and wound up with career totals of twelve interceptions, 105 unassisted tackles and eighty assists. He was named on every All-Big-Eight team in addition to a number of All-America first teams.

Clarence Scott tackles the Steelers' running back, Franco Harris.

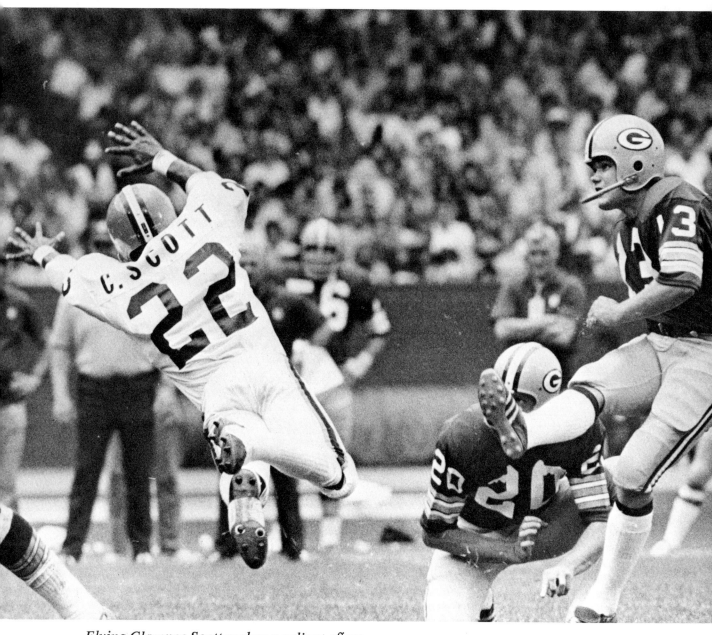

Flying Clarence Scott makes a valiant effort to block a field goal by Green Bay's Chester Marcol.

thom darden

Thom Darden, first choice of the Browns in the 1972 draft and a regular defensive back throughout that season, almost quit football before he really got started.

"When I was in high school I had a different attitude toward football," he recalled. "My first love was basketball. I thought I was a better basketball player than football player."

All the same, Darden was one of the stars of the Sandusky (Ohio) High School football team, and it was that sport that earned him a scholarship at the University of Michigan.

Michigan fans remember him for his interception in the last-minute victory over Ohio State in his senior year of 1971. He leapt over Dick Wakefield of the Buckeyes for what seemed like a miraculous theft.

Darden was tapped by the College All-Stars but still managed to play briefly in the Browns' opening exhibition against the Los Angeles Rams. The next week he was named to start at strong-side safety against the San Francisco 49ers and was a regular from that point on.

At six-foot-two and 195 pounds, Darden doesn't have dazzling speed but he does have an instinct for the catch. He made three interceptions during the 1972 season and returned those steals sixty-four-yards.

om Darden proved in 1972 that a rookie be just as devastating as an older er to an opponent's passing game.

105

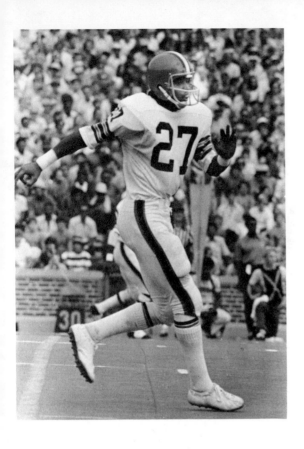

A Concensus All-American as a defensive back at Michigan University, Thom Darden has more than lived up to his college billings in the pros.

Thom Darden, tight safety, returns an interception against Detroit in 1972 exhibition play. The intended receiver on the play, Detroit's running back Mickey Zofko, vainly pursues Darden.

Safety Thom Darden breaks up a pass play to Detroit's Ron Jessie. His expert, if sometimes unorthodox, style of play made him team leader in interceptions in 1972.

Most coaches like to keep a rookie set at a position, but Nick Skorich showed his confidence in Darden by shifting him from strong-side to free safety during the season. His performance was equally effective.

Thom, a bright young man who has held an administrative post at John Carroll University in the offseason, found it difficult to adjust mentally when he first joined the Browns.

"The mental preparation was the most difficult thing," he states. "I never doubted that I could play physically. If you know the fundamentals you can play football.

"The difference is that you have to psyche yourself up with the pros. At Michigan the coach would get us up. The great professionals get themselves up each week. About the third game of the season I began to feel part of the Browns. Then I began to feel psyched up before every game."

charlie hall

Charlie Hall's family was in the stands at the Houston Astrodome on an October day in 1972 which made it a very happy homecoming for the Browns' second-year linebacker. The Cleveland team rallied to win and Charlie, a native of Yoakum, Texas, had his finest day as a pro.

The day started out brightly for Hall. The Oilers had attempted a pitchout but Hall reacted swiftly and jolted Robert Holmes for a nine-yard loss. Charlie, lean and quick at six-foot-three-and-a-half and 223 pounds, wound up that afternoon in Houston with eight unassisted tackles and four assists.

Drafted in the third round before the 1971 campaign, by the start of the 1972 season Hall had become a regular, but he shocked the coaches when he reported to camp at 205 pounds, far too low for a pro linebacker.

Charlie was advised to load up on steaks and milkshakes and to build himself up in any way he could. There were sighs of relief when he stepped on the scales six weeks later and pushed the indicator to 220 pounds.

He works on a weight-lifting program designed to strengthen his arms and shoulders, and which has helped him to put on some additional weight. Speed and quickness, however, are his big assets. He runs forty yards in 4.8 seconds.

Hall continued his improvement in 1973 and along with Bob Babich and John Garlington gave the team a strong linebacking corps.

Charlie Hall has established himself as a starter and a first-rate linebacker.

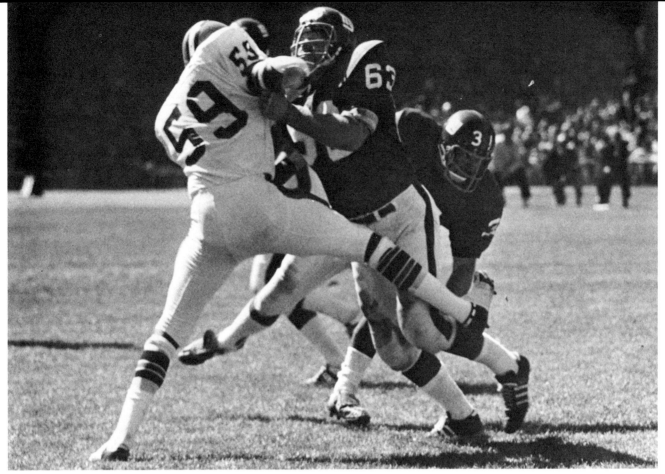

Linebacker Charlie Hall's chief assets are
speed and the ability to get off quickly.

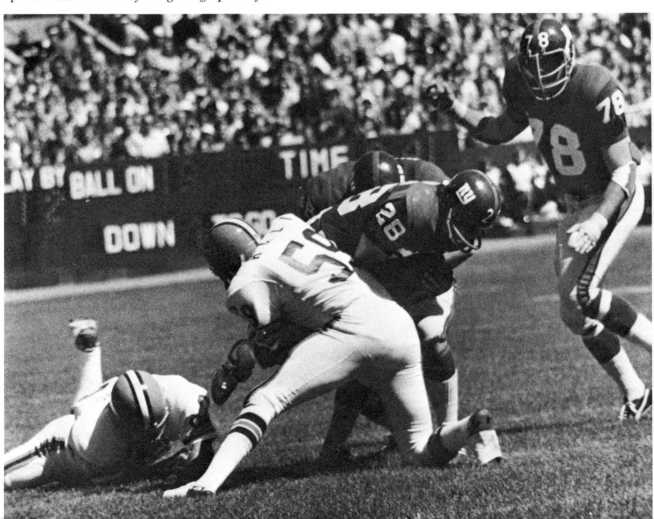

don cockroft

Nineteen seventy-two was a banner year for Cleveland kicker Don Cockroft. His fine performance in the dual role of place-kicker and punter won him the Golden Toe Award and a check for $1,000.

During the regular season Cockroft connected on twenty-two of twenty-seven field goal attempts. One was the fifty-seven-yarder against the Denver Broncos that set a new Browns' record. In 1973 he hit on twenty-two of thirty-one.

Don considers a much shorter kick as the prize boot of the 1972 season: the twenty-six-yard kick against the Pittsburgh Steelers that gave the Browns their victory and their biggest upset in many a season.

The young man from Fountain, Colorado, also handles all of the Browns' punting in an equally effective manner. He kicked the ball eighty-one times for a 43.2 yard average in 1972 and in 1973 he had a 40.5 average.

Don Cockroft attributes his improved performance to several factors. Special teams coach Al Tabor has devoted a lot of time instructing him. He was also spurred on in 1972 training by competition from rookie George Hunt. Furthermore, Cockroft is now in the best physical condition of his life.

Above all Don claims, "I am in the best spiritual shape of my life."

He feels this spiritual force has given him the strength and courage needed to do his best.

"In the past I was ready to give up anything to follow Christ except football," says Cockroft. "Now I can give up football."

That doesn't mean that he has retirement plans. "I would like to kick for as many years as I can," he adds. "But God has a plan for all of us. Being a Christian and accepting the Word of God as it is, I want to follow the plan. I don't know what the future holds." In the meantime he feels he's playing football with God's blessing.

Punter Don Cockroft follows the path of his booming kick as a Giant defender arrives too late.

Don Cockroft unleashes a long punt before Giant Rocky Thompson can stop it.

Former quarterback Don Gault holds for a Don Cockroft field goal attempt.

frank pitts

-e-handed Frank Pitts was the Browns'
-ding receiver in both 1972 and 1973,
-nering 67 passes in that time for 937
-ds.

Frank Pitts dashes around the field like a hot-rod on legs. In 1971 that was just what the Browns needed. Negotiations with the Kansas City Chiefs were in progress most of the summer of that year. Finally, Pitts was pried away from Hank Stram for a draft choice and the Browns have never regretted the deal.

Through the first eight weeks of the 1971 season, Frank was used sparingly. His total was three catches for thirty-seven yards. Pitts was moved into the starting lineup in place of Gary Collins in a game against his former team. He made five catches for 129 yards in that game and became a fixture in the Cleveland lineup.

The Phipps-to-Pitts passing combination has become one of the most feared in football. Frank wound up as the team's leading pass grabber in 1972 with thirty-six catches for 620 yards. He averaged 17.2 yards a catch and scored eight touchdowns.

He led the Browns again in 1973 with thirty-one catches for 317 yards.

The former Southern University athlete caught seventy-eight passes for 1,450 yards and eleven touchdowns in his three-year apprenticeship in Kansas City before blossoming into a real bomb threat in 1968. It was this ability that attracted Skorich.

Pitts, who is six-foot-two and 200 pounds, has been clocked at 9.5 seconds in the 100-yard dash. He likes to take the ball on the dead run but also has great leaping ability. He has given the Browns the outside speed they've needed at wide receiver.

Not only does Frank Pitts have great hands and speed, he is one of the best open-field runners in football. Here he steps around a fallen Bengal (above) and through a pile of fallen Patriot bodies (right) on his goalward path.

greg pruitt

The improved status of the Browns in the NFL was indicated in 1973 when two Cleveland players made the Pro Bowl squad. None had achieved that honor the previous year. Greg Pruitt made it in the kickoff and punt return department and Clarence Scott won a job as a cornerback. Pruitt, the mighty mite from Oklahoma, was one of three rookies so honored.

Greg was fourth among the Browns in rushing and he also scored five touchdowns. He led the team in kickoff and punt returns with 28.3 and 11.3 averages respectively.

Some members of the Cleveland coaching staff originally felt that Pruitt at five-foot-nine, 185 pounds was too small. Bob Nussbaumer, the team's personnel director, not only was convinced that Greg was a fine prospect but the best available. So the little Sooner, the thirtieth man to go in the draft, became Cleveland property.

Without Nussbaumer's strong endorsement, Pruitt's size might have kept him out of a Browns' uniform. The rookie, however, believes that being on the small side may have contributed to his success.

"A little guy has more incentive," he explains. "He has to go harder all the time. This developed my style of running which is to keep moving."

The speedster states he was clocked at Oklahoma at 4.4 for forty yards and at 6.1 for sixty yards saying, "I think you run as fast as you have to when you see that open field ahead."

Greg feels that his height can be an advantage as well as a disadvantage.

"Sometimes when I'm following a big tackle or guard, the tacklers don't even see me," he explains. "I sort of hide behind them. It works the other way, too. I have to be careful how I position myself so I can see what's out in front."

Pruitt is paid well on his long-term contract with the Browns but lives modestly. His agent has the halfback on a strict budget.

"I get enough to live on and he invests the rest," says Gregg.

The young bachelor lives alone in an apartment in a Cleveland suburb and says that "coming home tired and having to cook dinner isn't much fun," but he has had some experience in the culinary department. His parents were separated when he was about ten years old and his mother went to work in their hometown of Houston. "So I got my own meals part of the time," he recalls.

Most important, however, the Browns are more than satisfied with their big little man.

Because of his amazing speed, Greg Pruitt averaged almost ten yards per carry at the University of Oklahoma.

A Nelsen-to-Kelly handoff sends the Browns' and Colts' gears into motion.